VOCAL SELECTIONS FROM
ON THE
TWENTIETH
CENTURY

Music by CY COLEMAN
Lyrics by BETTY COMDEN and ADOLPH GREEN

ISBN 978-1-4234-9833-9

HAL•LEONARD®
CORPORATION
7777 W. BLUEMOUND RD. P.O. BOX 13819 MILWAUKEE, WI 53213

For info on Notable Music Co. Inc./The Cy Coleman Office, visit
www.cycoleman.com and **www.myspace.com/cycoleman**

Visit Hal Leonard Online at
www.halleonard.com

Cy Coleman

Cy Coleman was a musician's composer, classically trained at piano, composition, and orchestration at New York City's High School for the Performing Arts and NY College of Music. Mr. Coleman was being groomed to be the next great conductor. Instead he turned his passion to jazz and formed the popular Cy Coleman Trio. Born Seymour Kaufman on June 14, 1929 in the Bronx, he changed his name at age 16 in time to use it on his first compositions with lyricist Joe A. McCarthy ("Why Try to Change Me Now," and "I'm Gonna Laugh You Right Out of My Life"). While still performing in jazz clubs and enjoying a successful recording career, Cy began writing with veteran songwriter Carolyn Leigh. Hits like "Witchcraft" and "The Best Is Yet to Come" were followed by their leap to Broadway with *Wildcat,* starring Lucille Ball ("Hey, Look Me Over") and then *Little Me* ("I've Got Your Number" and "Real Live Girl"). In 1966 Cy, along with legendary lyricist Dorothy Fields, triumphed with the smash hit *Sweet Charity* ("Big Spender," "If My Friends Could See Me Now"). Cy continued on Broadway and wrote the scores for *Seesaw, I Love My Wife, On the Twentieth Century, Barnum, City of Angels, The Will Rogers Follies,* and *The Life.* In 2004 Cy returned to his roots and revived the Cy Coleman Trio, once again wowing the audiences with his amazing skill at the piano. In Mr. Coleman's amazing career he took home three Tony® Awards, two GRAMMY Awards®, three Emmy® Awards, an Academy Award® nomination, and countless honors. Cy served on the Board of ASCAP for three decades.

Contents

ON THE TWENTIETH CENTURY

Music by CY COLEMAN
Lyrics by BETTY COMDEN and ADOLPH GREEN

We point with the deep-est pride to the grand-est ride on the
Our heart with e-mo-tion reels when this prince of wheels starts to

New York Cen-tral Rail-road, The a-ris-to-crat of
make its dai-ly jour-ney, Ei-ther Chi — N. Y., or

I RISE AGAIN

Music by CY COLEMAN
Lyrics by BETTY COMDEN and ADOLPH GREEN

VERONIQUE

Music by CY COLEMAN
Lyrics by BETTY COMDEN and ADOLPH GREEN

19

OUR PRIVATE WORLD

Music by CY COLEMAN
Lyrics by BETTY COMDEN and ADOLPH GREEN

TOGETHER

Music by CY COLEMAN
Lyrics by BETTY COMDEN and ADOLPH GREEN

NEVER

Music by CY COLEMAN
Lyrics by BETTY COMDEN and ADOLPH GREEN

REPENT

Music by CY COLEMAN
Lyrics by BETTY COMDEN and ADOLPH GREEN

I'VE GOT IT ALL

Music by CY COLEMAN
Lyrics by BETTY COMDEN and ADOLPH GREEN

Deliberately

Life is sim - ply great, my sil - ver - wear is gold, Through
Chauf - feur, but - ler, cook, they're for - eign and they're old, Get

my Bel - air es - tate _____ cham - pagne's a flow - ing riv - er.
all my pic - tures took _____ by Mis - ter Ce - cil Bea - ton.

MINE

Music by CY COLEMAN
Lyrics by BETTY COMDEN and ADOLPH GREEN

FIVE ZEROS

Music by CY COLEMAN
Lyrics by BETTY COMDEN and ADOLPH GREEN

One, two, three, four, five. One, two, three, four,

Five Ze - ros pre - ce - ded by a two, pre - ce - ded by a dol - lar sign is

too, oh, oh, oh, oh, oh, won - der - ful for words.

Hel - lo, old friend, hel - lo, Mis - ter Mon - ey, you've been a - way so long, pull up a

soon you'll share the glo - ry when the thea - tre bursts with cheers!
keep my land - lord hap - py and you sweep a - way my fears.

Hel - lo, old friend, ___ Hel - lo, Mis - ter Broad mi -
Hel - lo, old friend, ___ Hel - lo, fi - let mi -

way, ___ You ain't seen noth - in' yet, ___ we're gon - na tear the town a - part.
gnon, ___ Hel - lo there, silk pa - ja - mas, which I ain't been wear - ing since ___

Hel - lo, old friend, ___ we're bring - ing back to Broad -
My long lost friend, ___ I love you, Mis - ter Mon -

SHE'S A NUT

Music by CY COLEMAN
Lyrics by BETTY COMDEN and ADOLPH GREEN

THE LEGACY

Music by CY COLEMAN
Lyrics by BETTY COMDEN and ADOLPH GREEN

You may feel bad for a-while, _____ but it's bet-ter far this way, _____ For I am much too good a show-man to dwin-dle like a snow-man melt-ing down some sun-ny day. _____ My of-fice

78

LIFE IS LIKE A TRAIN

Music by CY COLEMAN
Lyrics by BETTY COMDEN and ADOLPH GREEN

Clockwise: Kevin Kline, Imogene Coca,
John Cullum, Judy Kaye